ONENESS WITH ALL LIFE

ECKHART TOLLE

ONENESS WITH ALL LIFE

Awaken to a life of purpose and presence

MICHAEL JOSEPH
an imprint of
PENGUIN BOOKS

MICHAEL JOSEPH

UK | USA | Canada | Ireland | Australia
India | New Zealand | South Africa

Michael Joseph is part of the Penguin Random House group of companies
whose addresses can be found at global.penguinrandomhouse.com

First published in the United States of America by Dutton, a member of
Penguin Group (USA) Inc., and Namaste Publishing 2008

First published in Australia by Michael Joseph 2008
First published in Great Britain by Michael Joseph 2009
Published in this edition 2018

011

Set in 10.2/13.5 pt Stempel Garamond LT Pro
Typeset by Jouve (UK), Milton Keynes
Printed and bound in Great Britain by Clays Ltd, Elcograf S.p.A.

A CIP catalogue record for this book is available from the British Library

ISBN: 978-0-241-37382-8

www.greenpenguin.co.uk

MIX
Paper from
responsible sources
FSC® C018179

Penguin Random House is committed to a
sustainable future for our business, our readers
and our planet. This book is made from Forest
Stewardship Council® certified paper.

CONTENTS

INTRODUCTION

For this companion volume to A New Earth, I selected passages from the original book that felt particularly suitable for inspirational or meditative reading. For this reason I do not recommend that you read this book straight through from cover to cover. It would be far more beneficial to read, at the most, one chapter at a time, stopping at and perhaps rereading whatever passages elicit an inner response. Then let the words sink in and sense the truth to which they point, which is, of course, already within you. It can also be helpful to open the book at random occasionally, read one page or just one passage and let the words point the way to that dimension deep within that is beyond words, beyond thought. The truth to which the words point, the timeless dimension of consciousness, cannot be arrived at through discursive thought and conceptual understanding.

This book is not a condensed version of A New Earth. Although it contains some of the most powerful pointers from the original book, there is relatively little here about the ego and nothing about the pain-body. In other words: If you want to understand and thus be able to detect those mental-emotional patterns within you that block the arising of a new consciousness, you have to go to the original book.

This book will be of greatest benefit to those who have already read A New Earth – perhaps more than once – responded to it deeply, and experienced some degree of inner transformation through it. The informational content of this book is of relatively little importance. You read it not so much to learn something new, but to go deeper, become more present, awaken out of the stream of incessant and compulsive thinking. If there is no inner recognition, however distant or fleeting, of that to which the words point, then the words will be quite meaningless and remain no more than abstract concepts. If there is such a recognition, however, it means that the awakened consciousness is beginning to emerge from within you and the words you are reading help to draw it out. If you come across passages in this book that you feel are powerful, I want you to realize that what you are feeling is your own spiritual power, that is to say who you are in your essence. Only Spirit can recognize Spirit.

Chapter 1

GOING BEYOND
THOUGHT

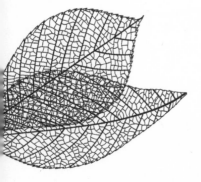

Thinking is no more than a tiny aspect of the totality of consciousness, the totality of who you are.

What is arising now is not a new belief system, a new religion, spiritual ideology, or mythology. We are coming to the end not only of mythologies but also of ideologies and belief systems. The change goes deeper than the content of your mind, deeper than your thoughts. In fact, at the heart of the new consciousness lies the transcendence of thought, the newfound ability of rising above thought, of realizing a dimension within yourself that is infinitely more vast than thought.

You then no longer derive your identity, your sense of who you are, from the incessant stream of thinking that in the old consciousness you take to be yourself. What a liberation to realize that the "voice in my head" is not who I am.

Who am I then? The one who sees that. The awareness that is prior to thought, the space in which the thought — or the emotion or sense perception — happens.

The primary cause of unhappiness is never the situation but your thoughts about it.

Be aware of the thoughts you are thinking. Separate them from the situation, which is always neutral, which always is as it is. There is the situation or the fact, and here are my thoughts about it. Instead of making up stories, stay with the facts. For example, "I am ruined" is a story. It limits you and prevents you from taking effective action. "I have fifty cents left in my bank account" is a fact. Facing facts is always empowering. Be aware that what you think, to a large extent, creates the emotions that you feel. See the link between your thinking and your emotions. Rather than being your thoughts and emotions, be the awareness behind them.

"The wisdom of this world is folly with God," says the Bible.[1] What is the wisdom of this world? The movement of thought, and meaning that is defined exclusively by thought.

Thinking isolates a situation or event and calls it good or bad, as if it had a separate existence. Through excessive reliance on thinking, reality becomes fragmented. This fragmentation is an illusion, but it seems very real while you are trapped in it. And yet the universe is an indivisible whole in which all things are interconnected, in which nothing exists in isolation. The deeper interconnectedness of all things and events implies that the mental labels of "good" and "bad" are ultimately illusory. They always imply a limited perspective and so are true only relatively and temporarily.

There are no random events, nor are there events or things that exist by and for themselves, in isolation. The atoms that make up your body were once forged inside stars, and the causes of even the smallest event are virtually infinite and connected with the whole in incomprehensible ways.

If you wanted to trace back the cause of any event, you would have to go back all the way to the beginning of creation. The cosmos is not chaotic. The very word *cosmos* means order. But this is not an order the human mind can ever comprehend, although it can sometimes glimpse it.

When we go into a forest that has not been interfered with by man, our thinking mind will see only disorder and chaos all around us. It won't even be able to differentiate between life (good) and death (bad) anymore since everywhere new life grows out of rotting and decaying matter. Only if we are still enough inside and the noise of thinking subsides can we become aware that there is a hidden harmony here, a sacredness, a higher order in which everything has its perfect place and could not be other than what it is and the way it is.

The mind is more comfortable in a landscaped park because it has been planned through thought; it has not grown organically. There is an order here that the mind can understand. In the forest, there is an incomprehensible order that to the mind looks like chaos. It is beyond the mental categories of good and bad. You cannot understand it through thought, but you can sense it when you let go of thought, become still and alert, and don't try to understand or explain. Only then can you be aware of the sacredness of the forest. As soon as you sense that hidden harmony, that sacredness, you realize you are not separate from it, and when you realize that, you become a conscious participant in it. In this way, nature can help you become realigned with the wholeness of life.

This is most people's reality: As soon as something is perceived, it is named, interpreted, compared with something else, liked, disliked, or called good or bad by the phantom self, the ego. They are imprisoned in thought forms, in object consciousness.

You do not awaken spiritually until the compulsive and unconscious naming ceases, or at least you become aware of it and thus are able to observe it as it happens. It is through this constant naming that the ego remains in place as the unobserved mind. Whenever it ceases and even when you just become aware of it, there is inner space, and you are not possessed by the mind anymore.

Choose an object close to you—a pen, a chair, a cup, a plant—and explore it visually, that is to say, look at it with great interest, almost curiosity. Avoid any objects with strong personal associations that remind you of the past, such as where you bought it, who gave it to you, and so on. Also avoid anything that has writing on it such as a book or a bottle. It would stimulate thought. Without straining, relaxed but alert, give your complete attention to the object, every detail of it. If thoughts arise, don't get involved in them. It is not the thoughts you are interested in, but the act of perception itself. Can you take the thinking out of the perceiving? Can you look without the voice in your head commenting, drawing conclusions, comparing, or trying to figure something out? After a couple of minutes or so, let your gaze wander around the room or wherever you are, your alert attention lighting up each thing that it rests upon.

Then, listen to any sounds that may be-present. Listen to them in the same way as you looked at the things around you. Some sounds may be natural—water, wind, birds—while others are man-made. Some may be pleasant, others unpleasant. However, don't differentiate between good and bad. Allow each sound to be as it is, without interpretation. Here too, relaxed but alert attention is the key.

When we perceive without interpreting or mental labeling, which means without adding thought to our perceptions, we can still sense the deeper connectedness underneath our perception of seemingly separate things.

See if you can catch, that is to say, notice, the voice in the head, perhaps in the very moment it complains about something, and recognize it for what it is: the voice of the ego, no more than a conditioned mind-pattern, a thought. Whenever you notice that voice, you will also realize that you are not the voice, but the one who is aware of it.

In fact, you *are* the awareness that is aware of the voice. In the background, there is the awareness. In the foreground, there is the voice, the thinker. In this way you are becoming free of the ego, free of the unobserved mind.

Neither concepts nor mathematical formulae can explain the infinite. No thought can encapsulate the vastness of the totality. Reality is a unified whole, but thought cuts it up into fragments. This gives rise to fundamental misperceptions, for example, that there are separate things and events, or that *this* is the cause of *that*. Every thought implies a perspective, and every perspective, by its very nature, implies limitation, which ultimately means that it is not true, at least not absolutely. Only the whole is true, but the whole cannot be spoken or thought. Seen from beyond the limitations of thinking and therefore incomprehensible to the human mind, everything is happening now. All that ever has been or will be is now, outside of time, which is a mental construct.

When you don't cover up the world with words and labels, a sense of the miraculous returns to your life that was lost a long time ago when humanity, instead of using thought, became possessed by thought. A depth returns to your life. Things regain their newness, their freshness. And the greatest miracle is the experiencing of your essential self as prior to any words, thoughts, mental labels, and images. For this to happen, you need to disentangle your sense of I, of Beingness, from all the things it has become mixed up with, that is to say, identified with.

Is it possible to let go of the belief that you should or need to know who you are? In other words, can you cease looking to conceptual definitions to give you a sense of self? Can you cease looking to *thought* for an identity?

The more you make your thoughts into your identity, the more cut off you are from the spiritual dimension within yourself.

Defining yourself through thought is limiting yourself. When you fully accept that you don't know, you actually enter a state of peace and clarity that is closer to who you truly are than thought could ever be.

Don't seek happiness. If you seek it, you won't find it, because seeking is the antithesis of happiness. Happiness is ever elusive, but freedom from unhappiness is attainable now, by facing what is rather than making up stories about it. Unhappiness covers up your natural state of well-being and inner peace, the source of true happiness.

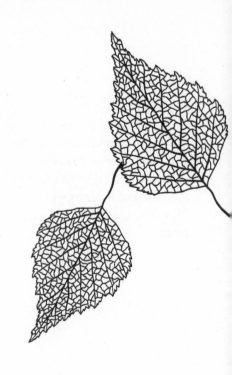

Chapter 2

THE POWER OF THE
PRESENT MOMENT

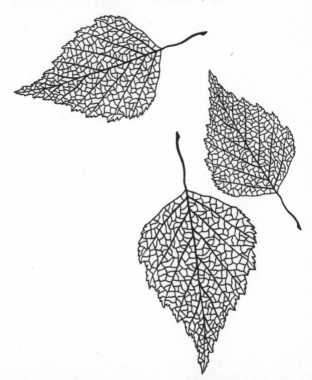

The ego's greatest enemy is the present moment, which is to say, life itself.

Time is seen as the endless succession of moments, some "good," some "bad." Yet, if you look more closely, that is to say, through your own immediate experience, you find that there are not many moments at all. You discover that there is only ever *this moment*. Life is always now. Your entire life unfolds in this constant Now. Even past or future moments only exist when you remember or anticipate them, and you do so by thinking about them in the only moment there is: this one.

Why does it appear then as if there were many moments? Because the present moment is confused with what happens, confused with content. The space of Now is confused with what happens in that space. The confusion of the present moment with content gives rise not only to the illusion of time, but also the illusion of ego.

Everything seems to be subject to time, yet it all happens in the Now. That is the paradox. Wherever you look, there is plenty of *circumstantial* evidence for the reality of time—a rotting apple, your face in the bathroom mirror compared to your face in a photo taken thirty years ago—yet you never find any *direct* evidence, you never experience time itself. You only ever experience the present moment, or rather what happens in it. If you go by direct evidence only, there is no time, and the Now is all there ever is.

Whatever is or happens is the form that the Now takes. As long as you resist it internally, form, that is to say, the world, is an impenetrable barrier that separates you from who you are beyond form, separates you from the formless one Life that you are. When you bring an inner yes to the form the Now takes, that very form becomes a doorway into the formless. The separation between the world and God dissolves.

If you resist what happens, you are at the mercy of what happens, and the world will determine your happiness and unhappiness.

Most egos have conflicting wants. They want different things at different times or may not even know what they want except that they don't want what is: the present moment.

To be in alignment with *what is* means to be in a relationship of inner nonresistance with what happens. It means not to label it mentally as good or bad, but to let it be. Does this mean you can no longer take action to bring about change in your life? On the contrary. When the basis for your actions is inner alignment with the present moment, your actions become empowered by the intelligence of Life itself.

Whenever you become anxious or stressed, outer purpose has taken over, and you lost sight of your inner purpose. You have forgotten that your state of consciousness is primary, all else secondary.

Why do anxiety, stress, or negativity arise? Because you turned away from the present moment. And why did you do that? You thought something else was more important. You forgot your main purpose. One small error, one misperception, creates a world of suffering.

There are three ways in which the ego will treat the present moment: as a means to and end, as an obstacle, or as an enemy.

When you react against the form that Life takes at this moment, when you treat the Now as a means, an obstacle, or an enemy, you strengthen your own form identity, the ego. Hence the ego's reactivity. What is reactivity? Becoming addicted to reaction. The more reactive you are, the more entangled you become with form. The more identified with form, the stronger the ego. Your Being then does not shine through form anymore—or only barely.

People believe themselves to be dependent on what happens for their happiness, that is to say, dependent on form. They don't realize that what happens is the most unstable thing in the universe. It changes constantly. They look upon the present moment as either marred by something that has happened and shouldn't have or as deficient because of something that has not happened but should have. And so they miss the deeper perfection that is inherent in life itself, a perfection that is always already here, that lies beyond what is happening or not happening, beyond form.

Accept the present moment and find the perfection that is deeper than any form and untouched by time.

The most important, the primordial relationship in your life is your relationship with the Now, or rather with whatever form the Now takes, that is to say, what is or what happens. If your relationship with the Now is dysfunctional, that dysfunction will be reflected in every relationship and every situation you encounter. The ego could be defined simply in this way: a dysfunctional relationship with the present moment. It is at this moment that you can decide what kind of relationship you want to have with the present moment.

"Do I want the present moment to be my friend or my enemy?" The present moment is inseparable from life, so you are really deciding what kind of relationship you want to have with life. Once you have decided you want the present moment to be your friend, it is up to you to make the first move: Become friendly toward it, welcome it no matter in what disguise it comes, and soon you will see the results. Life becomes friendly toward you; people become helpful, circumstances cooperative. One decision changes your entire reality. But that one decision you have to make again and again and again—until it becomes natural to live in such a way.

The elimination of time from your consciousness is the elimination of ego. It is the only true spiritual practice . . . What we are speaking of is the elimination of *psychological* time, which is the egoic mind's endless pre-occupation with past and future and its unwillingness to be one with life by living in alignment with the inevitable *isness* of the present moment.

Whenever a habitual no to life turns into a yes, whenever you allow this moment to be as it is, you dissolve time as well as ego. For the ego to survive, it must make time—past and future—more important than the present moment.

Time is the horizontal dimension of life, the surface layer of reality. Then there is the vertical dimension of depth, accessible to you only through the portal of the present moment.

Your secondary or outer purpose lies within the dimension of time, while your main purpose is inseparable from the Now and therefore requires the negation of time. How are they reconciled? By realizing that your entire life journey ultimately consists of the step your are taking at this moment. There is always only this one step, and you give it your fullest attention. This doesn't mean you don't know where you are going; it just means this step is primary, the destination secondary. And what you encounter at your destination once you get there depends on the quality of this one step. Another way of putting it: What the future holds for you depends on your state of consciousness now.

Through the present moment, you have access to the power of life itself, that which has traditionally been called "God." As soon as you turn away from it, God ceases to be a reality in your life, and all you are left with is the mental concept of God, which some people believe in and others deny. Even belief in God is only a poor substitute for the living reality of God manifesting every moment of your life.

Chapter 3

WHO AM I

The ultimate truth of who you are is not I am this or I am that, but I Am.

E quating the physical sense-perceived body with "I," the body that is destined to grow old, wither, and die, always leads to suffering sooner or later. To refrain from identifying with the body doesn't mean that you neglect, despise, or no longer care for it. If it is strong, beautiful, or vigorous, you can enjoy and appreciate those attributes — while they last. You can also improve the body's condition through right nutrition and exercise. If you don't equate the body with who you are, when beauty fades, vigor diminishes, or the body becomes incapacitated, this will not affect your sense of worth or identity in any way. In fact, as the body begins to weaken, the formless dimension, the light of consciousness, can shine more easily through the fading form.

Ego arises when your sense of Beingness, of "I Am," which is formless consciousness, gets mixed up with form. This is the meaning of identification. This is forgetfulness of Being, the primary error, the illusion of absolute separateness that turns reality into a nightmare.

Ego is always identification with form, seeking yourself and thereby losing yourself in some form. Forms are not just material objects and physical bodies. More fundamental than the external forms—things and bodies—are the thought forms that continuously arise in the field of consciousness.

You are a human being. What does that mean? Mastery of life is not a question of control, but of finding a balance between human and Being. Mother, father, husband, wife, young, old, the roles you play, the functions you fulfill, whatever you do—all that belongs to the human dimension. It has its place and needs to be honored, but in itself it is not enough for a fulfilled, truly meaningful relationship or life. Human alone is never enough, no matter how hard you try or what you achieve. Then there is Being. It is found in the still, alert presence of Consciousness itself, the Consciousness that you are. Human is form. Being is formless. Human and Being are not separate but interwoven.

When you become aware of the transience of all forms, your attachment to them lessens, and you disidentify from them to some extent. Being detached does not mean that you cannot enjoy the good that the world has to offer. In fact, you enjoy it more. Once you see and accept the transience of all things and the inevitability of change, you can enjoy the pleasures of the world while they last without fear of loss or anxiety about the future. When you are detached, you gain a higher vantage point from which to view the events in your life instead of being trapped inside them.

"Blessed are the poor in spirit," Jesus said, "for theirs is the kingdom of heaven."[2] What does "poor in spirit" mean? No inner baggage, no identifications. Not with things, nor with any mental concepts that have a sense of self in them. And what is the "kingdom of heaven"? The simple but profound joy of Being that is there when you let go of identifications and so become "poor in spirit."

How do you let go of attachment to things? Don't even try. It's impossible. Attachment to things drops away by itself when you no longer seek to find yourself in them. In the meantime, just be aware of your attachment to things. Sometimes you may not know that you are attached to something, which is to say, identified, until you lose it or there is the threat of loss. If you then become upset, anxious, and so on, it means you are attached. If you are aware that you are identified with a thing, the identification is no longer total. "I am the awareness that is aware that there is attachment." That's the beginning of the transformation of consciousness.

When you contemplate the unfathomable depth of space or listen to the silence in the early hours just before sunrise, something within you resonates with it as if in recognition. You then sense the vast depth of space as your own depth, and you know that precious stillness that has no form to be more deeply who you are than any of the things that make up the content of your life.

The twofold reality of the universe, which consists of things and space—thingness and no-thingness—is also your own. A sane, balanced, and fruitful human life is a dance between the two dimensions that make up reality: form and space. Most people are so identified with the dimension of form, with sense perceptions, thoughts, and emotions, that the vital hidden half is missing from their lives. Their identification with form keeps them trapped in ego.

Just as space enables all things to exist and just as without silence there could be no sound, you would not exist without the vital formless dimension that is the essence of who you are. We could say "God" if the word had not been so misused. I prefer to call it Being. Being is prior to existence. Existence is form, content, "what happens." Existence is the foreground of life; Being is the background, as it were.

The collective disease of humanity is that people are so engrossed in what happens, so hypnotized by the world of fluctuating forms, so absorbed in the content of their lives, they have forgotten the essence, that which is beyond content, beyond form, beyond thought. They are so consumed by time that they have forgotten eternity, which is their origin, their home, their destiny. Eternity is the living reality of who you are.

Seeing beauty in a flower can awaken you, however briefly, to the beauty that is an essential part of your own innermost being, your true nature. Joy and love are intrinsically connected to that recognition. Flowers can become for us an expression in form of that which is most high, most sacred, and ultimately formless within ourselves. Flowers, more fleeting, more ethereal, and more delicate than the plants out of which they emerge, are like messengers from another realm, like a bridge between the world of physical forms and the formless. They not only have a scent that is delicate and pleasing, but also bring a fragrance from the realm of spirit.

When you are alert and contemplate a flower without naming it mentally, it becomes a window for you into the formless. There is an inner opening, however slight, into the spiritual dimension.

When you don't play roles, it means there is no self (ego) in what you do. There is no secondary agenda: protection or strengthening of your self. As a result, your actions have far greater power. You are totally focused on the situation. You become one with it. You don't try to be anybody in particular. You are most powerful, most effective, when you are completely yourself.

"How can I be myself?" is, however, the wrong question. It implies you have to do something to be yourself. But how doesn't apply here because you are yourself already. Just stop adding unnecessary baggage to who you already are. "But I don't know who I am. I don't know what it means to be myself." If you can be absolutely comfortable with not knowing who you are, then what's left is who you are—the Being behind the human, a field of pure potentiality rather than something that is already defined.

Give up defining yourself—to yourself or to others. You won't die. You will come to life. And don't be concerned with how others define you. When they define you, they are limiting themselves, so it's their problem. Whenever you interact with people, don't be there primarily as a function or a role, but as a field of conscious Presence.

When you react against the form that Life takes at this moment, when you treat the Now as a means, an obstacle, or an enemy, you strengthen your own form identity, the ego. Hence the ego's reactivity. What is reactivity? Becoming addicted to reaction. The more reactive you are, the more entangled you become with form. The more identified with form, the stronger the ego. Your Being then does not shine through form anymore—or only barely.

Through nonresistance to form, that in you which is beyond form emerges as an all-encompassing Presence, a silent power far greater than your short-lived form identity, the person. It is more deeply who you are than anything in the world of form.

When you think, feel, perceive, and experience, consciousness is born into form. It is reincarnating—into a thought, a feeling, a sense perception, an experience. The cycle of rebirths that Buddhists hope to get out of eventually is happening continuously, and it is only at this moment—through the power of Now—that you can get out of it. Through complete acceptance of the form of the Now, you become internally aligned with space, which is the essence of Now. Through acceptance, you become spacious inside. Aligned with space instead of form: That brings true perspective and balance into your life.

People believe themselves to be dependent on what happens for their happiness, that is to say, dependent on form. They don't realize that what happens is the most unstable thing in the universe. It changes constantly. They look upon the present moment as either marred by something that has happened and shouldn't have or as deficient because of something that has not happened but should have. And so they miss the deeper perfection that is inherent in life itself, a perfection that is always already here, that lies beyond what is happening or not happening, beyond form. Accept the present moment and find the perfection that is deeper than any form and untouched by time.

The joy of Being, which is the only true happiness, cannot come to you through any form, possession, achievement, person, or event—through anything that happens. That joy cannot come to you—ever. It emanates from the formless dimension within you, from consciousness itself and thus is one with who you are.

Chapter 4

AWAKENING

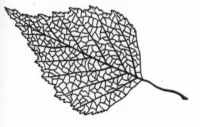

Only by awakening can you know the true meaning of that word.

Instead of being lost in your thinking, when you awaken you recognize yourself as the awareness behind it. Thinking then ceases to be a selfserving autonomous activity that takes possession of you and runs your life. Awareness takes over from thinking. Instead of being in charge of your life, thinking becomes the servant of awareness. Awareness is conscious connection with universal intelligence. Another word for it is Presence: consciousness without thought.

What is the relationship between awareness and thinking? Awareness is the space in which thoughts exist when that space has become conscious of itself.

Your inner purpose is to awaken. It is as simple as that. You share that purpose with every other person on the planet—because it is the purpose of humanity. Your inner purpose is an essential part of the purpose of the whole, the universe and its emerging intelligence. Your outer purpose can change over time. It varies greatly from person to person. Finding and living in alignment with the inner purpose is the foundation for fulfilling your outer purpose. It is the basis for true success.

Humanity is destined to go beyond suffering, but not in the way the ego thinks. One of the ego's many erroneous assumptions, one of its many deluded thoughts is "I should not have to suffer." That thought itself lies at the root of suffering. Suffering has a noble purpose: the evolution of consciousness (the awakening) and the burning up of the ego. The man on the cross is an archetypal image. He is every man and every woman. As long as you resist suffering, it is a slow process because the resistance creates more ego to burn up. When you accept suffering, however, there is an acceleration of that process which is brought about by the fact that you suffer consciously. You can accept suffering for yourself, or you can accept it for someone else, such as your child or parent. In the midst of conscious suffering, there is already the transmutation. The fire of suffering becomes the light of consciousness.

The ego says, "I shouldn't have to suffer," and that thought makes you suffer so much more. It is a distortion of the truth, which is always paradoxical. The truth is that you need to say yes to suffering before you can transcend it.

If the egoic earth drama has any purpose at all, it is an indirect one: It creates more and more suffering on the planet, and suffering, although largely ego-created, is in the end also ego-destructive. It is the fire in which the ego burns itself up.

"One day I will be free of the ego: I will awaken." Who is talking? The ego. To become free of the ego is not really a big job but a very small one. All you need to do is be aware of your thoughts and emotions—as they happen. This is not really a "doing," but an alert "seeing." In that sense, it is true that there is nothing you can do to become free of the ego. When that shift happens, which is the shift from thinking to awareness, an intelligence far greater than the ego's cleverness begins to operate in your life.

You do not become good by trying to be good, but by finding the goodness that is already within you, and allowing that goodness to emerge. But it can only emerge if something fundamental changes in your state of consciousness.

In Zen they say: "Don't seek the truth. Just cease to cherish opinions." What does that mean? Let go of identification with your mind. Who you are beyond the mind then emerges by itself.

An essential part of awakening is the recognition of the unawakened you, the ego as it thinks, speaks, and acts. When you recognize the unconsciousness in you, that which makes the recognition possible is the arising consciousness, is awakening. You cannot fight against the ego and win, just as you cannot fight against darkness. The light of consciousness is all that is necessary. You are that light.

A large part of many people's lives is consumed by an obsessive preoccupation with things. Whatever the ego seeks and gets attached to are substitutes for the Being that it cannot feel. You can value and care for things, but whenever you get attached to them, you will know it's the ego. And you are never really attached to a thing but to a thought that has "I," "me," or "mine" in it. Whenever you completely accept a loss, you go beyond ego, and who you are, the I Am which is consciousness itself, emerges.

Many people don't realize until they are on their deathbed and everything external falls away that nothing ever had anything to do with who they are. In the proximity of death, the whole concept of ownership stands revealed as ultimately meaningless. In the last moments of their life, they then also realize that while they were looking throughout their lives for a more complete sense of self, what they were really looking for, their Being, had actually always already been there, but had been largely obscured by their identification with things, which ultimately means identification with their mind.

For some, the awakening happens as they suddenly become aware of the kinds of thoughts they habitually think, especially persistent negative thoughts that they may have been identified with all of their lives. Suddenly there is an awareness that is aware of the thought but is not part of it.

The return movement in a person's life, the weakening or dissolution of form, whether through old age, illness, disability, loss, or some kind of personal tragedy, carries great potential for spiritual awakening—the dis-identification of consciousness from form.

On the new earth, old age will be universally recognized and highly valued as a time for the flowering of consciousness. For those who are still lost in the outer circumstances of their lives, it will be a time of a late homecoming, when they awaken to their inner purpose. For many others, it will represent an intensification and a culmination of the awakening process.

However, as your awareness increases and the ego is no longer running your life, you don't have to wait for your world to shrink or collapse through old age or personal tragedy in order for you to awaken to your inner purpose. As the new consciousness is beginning to emerge on the planet, an increasing number of people no longer need to be shaken to have an awakening. They embrace the awakening process voluntarily even while still engaged in the outward cycle of growth and expansion. When that cycle is no longer usurped by the ego, the spiritual dimension will come into this world through the outward movement—thought, speech, action, creation—as powerfully as through the return movement—stillness, Being, and the dissolution of form.

To love is to recognize yourself in another. The other's "otherness" then stands revealed as an illusion pertaining to the purely human realm, the realm of form.

When another recognizes you, that recognition draws the dimension of Being more fully into this world through both of you. That is the love that redeems the world.

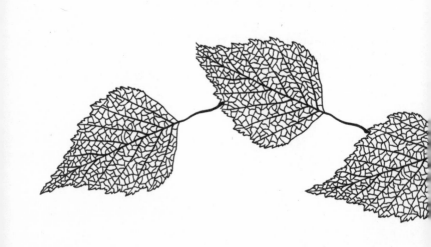

Chapter 5

INNER SPACE

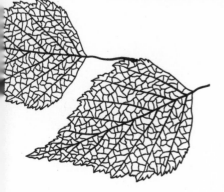

When consciousness is no longer totally absorbed by thinking, some of it remains in its formless, unconditioned, original state. This is inner space.

M ost people's lives are cluttered up with things: material things, things to do, things to think about. Their lives are like the history of humanity, which Winston Churchill defined as "one damn thing after another." Their minds are filled up with the clutter of thoughts, one thought after another. This is the dimension of object consciousness that is many people's predominant reality, and that is why their lives are so out of balance. Object consciousness needs to be balanced by space consciousness for sanity to return to our planet and for humanity to fulfill its destiny. The arising of space consciousness is the next stage in the evolution of humanity.

Space consciousness means that in addition to being conscious of things—which always comes down to sense perceptions, thoughts, and emotions—there is an undercurrent of awareness. Awareness implies that you are not only conscious of things (objects), but you are also conscious of being conscious. If you can sense an alert inner stillness in the background while things happen in the foreground—that's it! This dimension is there in everyone, but most people are completely unaware of it. Sometimes I point to it by saying, "Can you feel your own Presence?"

Space consciousness represents not only freedom from ego, but also from dependency on the things of this world, from materialism and materiality. It is the spiritual dimension which alone can give transcendent and true meaning to this world.

When you are no longer totally identified with forms, consciousness—who you are—becomes freed from its imprisonment in form. This freedom is the arising of inner space. It comes as a stillness, a subtle peace deep within you, even in the face of something seemingly bad. Suddenly, there is space around the event. There is also space around the emotional highs and lows, even around pain. And above all, there is space between your thoughts. And from that space emanates a peace that is not "of this world," because this world is form, and the peace is space. This is the peace of God.

Now you can enjoy and honor the things of this world without giving them an importance and significance they don't have. You can participate in the dance of creation and be active without attachment to outcome and without placing unreasonable demands upon the world: Fulfill me, make me happy, make me feel safe, tell me who I am. The world cannot give you those things, and when you no longer have such expectations, all self-created suffering comes to an end. All such suffering is due to an overvaluation of form and an unawareness of the dimension of inner space. When that dimension is present in your life, you can enjoy things, experiences, and the pleasures of the senses without losing yourself in them, without inner attachment to them, that is to say, without becoming addicted to the world.

When the dimension of space is lost or rather not known, the things of the world assume an absolute importance, a seriousness and heaviness that in truth they do not have. When the world is not viewed from the perspective of the formless, it becomes a threatening place, and ultimately a place of despair. The Old Testament prophet must have felt this when he wrote, "All things are full of weariness. A man cannot utter it."[3]

Discover inner space by creating gaps in the stream of thinking. Without those gaps, your thinking becomes repetitive, uninspired, devoid of any creative spark, which is how it still is for most people on the planet. You don't need to be concerned with the duration of those gaps. A few seconds is good enough. Gradually, they will lengthen by themselves, without any effort on your part. More important than their length is to bring them in frequently so that your daily activities and your stream of thinking become interspersed with space.

B e aware of your breathing. Notice how this takes attention away from your thinking and creates space.

Notice the sensation of the breath. Feel the air moving in and out of your body. Notice how the chest and abdomen expand and contract slightly with the in- and outbreath. One conscious breath is enough to make some space where before there was the uninterrupted succession of one thought after another. One conscious breath (two or three would be even better), taken many times a day, is an excellent way of bringing space into your life. Even if you meditated on your breathing for two hours or more, which some people do, one breath is all you ever need to be aware of, indeed ever can be aware of. The rest is memory or anticipation, which is to say, thought. Breathing isn't really something that you do but something that you witness as it happens. Breathing happens by itself. The intelligence within the body is doing it. All you have to do is watch it happening. There is no strain or effort involved. Also, notice the brief cessation of the breath, particularly the still point at the end of the outbreath, before you start breathing in again.

Whenever you are upset about an event, a person, or a situation, the real cause is not the event, person, or situation but a loss of true perspective that only space can provide. You are trapped in object consciousness, unaware of the timeless inner space of consciousness itself.

Space consciousness has little to do with being "spaced out." Both states are beyond thought. This they have in common. The fundamental difference, however, is that in the former, you rise above thought; in the latter, you fall below it. One is the next step in the evolution of human consciousness, the other a regression to a stage we left behind eons ago.

The greatest impediment to the discovery of inner space, the greatest impediment to finding the experiencer, the formless I Am, is to become so enthralled by the experience that you lose yourself in it. It means consciousness is lost in its own dream. You get taken in by every thought, every emotion, and every experience to such a degree that you are in fact in a dreamlike state. This has been the normal state of humanity for thousands of years.

When you hear of inner space, you may start seeking it, and, because you are seeking it as if you were looking for an object or for an experience, you cannot find it. This is the dilemma of all those who are seeking spiritual realization or enlightenment. Hence, Jesus said, "The kingdom of God is not coming with signs to be observed; nor will they say, 'Lo, here it is!' or 'There!' for behold, the kingdom of God is in the midst of you."[4]

If you are not spending all of your waking life in discontent, worry, anxiety, depression, despair, or consumed by other negative states; if you are able to enjoy simple things like listening to the sound of the rain or the wind; if you can see the beauty of clouds moving across the sky or be alone at times without feeling lonely or needing the mental stimulus of entertainment; if you find yourself treating a complete stranger with heartfelt kindness without wanting anything from him or her . . . it means that a space has opened up, no matter how briefly, in the otherwise incessant stream of thinking that is the human mind. When this happens, there is a sense of well-being, of alive peace, even though it may be subtle. The intensity will vary from a perhaps barely noticeable background sense of contentment to what the ancient sages of India called *ananda* — the bliss of Being. Because you have been conditioned to pay attention only to form, you are probably not aware of it except indirectly. For example, there is a common element in the ability to see beauty, to appreciate simple things, to enjoy your own company, or to relate to other people with loving kindness. This common element is a sense of contentment, peace, and aliveness that is the invisible background without which these experiences would not be possible.

Whenever there is beauty, kindness, the recognition of the goodness of simple things in your life, look for the background to that experience within yourself. But don't look for it as if you were looking for something. You cannot pin it down and say, "Now I have it," or grasp it mentally and define it in some way. It is like the cloudless sky. It has no form. It is space; it is stillness, the sweetness of Being and infinitely more than these words, which are only pointers. When you are able to sense it directly within yourself, it deepens. So when you appreciate something simple—a sound, a sight, a touch—when you see beauty, when you feel loving kindness toward another, sense the inner spaciousness that is the source and background to that experience.

Here is another way of finding inner space: Become conscious of being conscious. Say or think "I Am" and add nothing to it. Be aware of the stillness that follows the I Am. Sense your presence, the naked, unveiled, unclothed beingness. It is untouched by young or old, rich or poor, good or bad, or any other attributes.

Chapter 6

YOUR LIFE PURPOSE

Your life has an inner purpose and an outer purpose. Inner purpose concerns Being and is primary. Outer purpose concerns doing and is secondary.

The true or primary purpose of your life cannot be found on the outer level. It does not concern what you do but what you are—that is to say, your state of consciousness.

Action, although necessary, is only a secondary factor in manifesting our external reality. The primary factor in creation is consciousness. No matter how active we are, how much effort we make, our state of consciousness creates our world, and if there is no change on that inner level, no amount of action will make any difference. We would only re-create modified versions of the same world again and again, a world that is an external reflection of the ego.

Once you have had a glimpse of awareness or Presence, you know it firsthand. It is no longer just a concept in your mind. You can then make a conscious choice to be present rather than to indulge in useless thinking. You can invite Presence into your life, that is to say, make space. With the grace of awakening comes responsibility. You can either try to go on as if nothing has happened, or you can see its significance and recognize the arising of awareness as the most important thing that *can* happen to you. Opening yourself to the emerging consciousness and bringing its light into this world then becomes the primary purpose of your life.

Awakened doing is the alignment of your outer purpose—what you do—with your inner purpose—awakening and staying awake. Through awakened doing, you become one with the outgoing purpose of the universe. Consciousness flows through you into this world. It flows into your thoughts and inspires them. It flows into what you do and guides and empowers it.

The modalities of awakened doing are acceptance, enjoyment, and enthusiasm. Each one represents a certain vibrational frequency of consciousness. You need to be vigilant to make sure that one of them operates whenever you are engaged in doing anything at all—from the most simple task to the most complex. If you are not in the state of either acceptance, enjoyment, or enthusiasm, look closely and you will find that you are creating suffering for yourself and others.

Whatever you cannot enjoy doing, you can at least accept that this is what you have to do. Acceptance means: For now, this is what this situation, this moment requires me to do, and so I do it willingly.

If you can neither enjoy nor bring acceptance to what you do — stop. Otherwise, you are not taking responsibility for the only thing you can really take responsibility for, which also happens to be the one thing that really matters: your state of consciousness. And if you are not taking responsibility for your state of consciousness, you are not taking responsibility for life.

On the new earth, enjoyment will replace wanting as the motivating power behind people's actions. Wanting arises from the ego's delusion that you are a separate fragment that is disconnected from the power that lies behind all creation. Through enjoyment, you link into that universal creative power itself.

Expansion and positive change on the outer level is much more likely to come into your life if you can enjoy what you are doing already, instead of waiting for some change so that you can start enjoying what you do.

When you make the present moment, instead of past and future, the focal point of your life, your ability to enjoy what you do—and with it the quality of your life—increases dramatically.

Joy does not come from what you do, it flows into what you do and thus into this world from deep within you.

You will enjoy any activity in which you are fully present, any activity that is not just a means to an end. It isn't the action you perform that you really enjoy, but the deep sense of aliveness that flows into it. That aliveness is one with who you are. This means that when you enjoy doing something, you are really experiencing the joy of Being in its dynamic aspect. That's why anything you enjoy doing connects you with the power behind all creation.

Here is a spiritual practice that will bring empowerment and creative expansion into your life. Make a list of a number of everyday routine activities that you perform frequently. Include activities that you may consider uninteresting, boring, tedious, irritating, or stressful. But don't include anything that you hate or detest doing. That's a case either for acceptance or for stopping what you do. The list may include traveling to and from work, buying groceries, doing your laundry, or anything that you find tedious or stressful in your daily work. Then, whenever you are engaged in those activities, let them be a vehicle for alertness. Be absolutely present in what you do and sense the alert, alive stillness within you in the background of the activity. You will soon find that what you do in such a state of heightened awareness, instead of being stressful, tedious, or irritating, is actually becoming enjoyable. To be more precise, what you are enjoying is not really the outward action but the inner dimension of consciousness that flows into the action. This is finding the joy of Being in what you are doing. If you feel your life lacks significance or is too stressful or tedious, it is because you haven't brought that dimension into your life yet. Being conscious in what you do has not yet become your main aim.

Enthusiasm means there is deep enjoyment in what you do plus the added element of a goal or vision that you work toward. When you add a goal to the enjoyment of what you do, the energy-field or vibrational frequency changes. A certain degree of what we might call structural tension is now added to enjoyment, and so it turns into enthusiasm. At the height of creative activity fueled by enthusiasm, there will be enormous intensity and energy behind what you do. You will feel like an arrow that is moving toward the target—and enjoying the journey.

To an onlooker, it may appear that you are under stress, but the intensity of enthusiasm has nothing to do with stress. When you want to arrive at your goal more than you want to be doing what you are doing, you become stressed. The balance between enjoyment and structural tension is lost, and the latter has won.

Stress always diminishes both the quality and effectiveness of what you do under its influence. There is also a strong link between stress and negative emotions, such as anxiety and anger. Stress is also toxic to the body.

U nlike stress, enthusiasm has a high energy frequency and so resonates with the creative power of
the universe. This is why Ralph Waldo Emerson said that,
"Nothing great has ever been achieved without enthusiasm."[5]

E nthusiasm knows where it is going, but at the same
time, it is deeply at one with the present moment,
the source of aliveness, its joy, and its power. Enthusiasm
"wants" nothing because it lacks nothing. It is at one with
life and no matter how dynamic the enthusiasm-inspired
activities are, you don't lose yourself in them. And there
remains always a still but intensely alive space at the
center of the wheel, a core of peace in the midst of activity that is both the source of all and untouched by it all.

We are in the midst of a momentous event in the evolution of human consciousness. On our planet, and perhaps simultaneously in many parts of our galaxy and beyond, consciousness is awakening from the dream of form. This does not mean all forms (the world) are going to dissolve, although quite a few almost certainly will. It means consciousness can now begin to create form without losing itself in it. It can remain conscious of itself, even while it creates and experiences form. Why should it continue to create and experience form? For the enjoyment of it. How does consciousness do that? Through awakened humans who have learned the meaning of *awakened doing.*

A new species is arising on the planet. It is arising now, and you are it!

Chapter 7

BECOMING PRESENT

We can learn not to keep situations or events alive in our minds, but to return our attention continuously to the pristine, timeless present moment rather than be caught up in mental movie-making. Our very Presence then becomes our identity, rather than our thoughts and emotions.

Only Presence can free you of the ego, and you can only be present Now, not yesterday or tomorrow. Only Presence can undo the past in you and thus transform your state of consciousness.

Be alert. If there is awareness in you, you will be able to recognize the voice in your head for what it is: an old thought, conditioned by the past. If there is awareness in you, you no longer need to believe in every thought you think. It's an old thought, no more. Awareness means Presence, and only Presence can dissolve the unconscious past in you.

What in Zen is called *satori* is a moment of Presence, a brief stepping out of the voice in your head, the thought processes, and their reflection in the body as emotion. It is the arising of inner spaciousness where before there was the clutter of thought and the turmoil of emotion.

To end the misery that has afflicted the human condition for thousands of years, you have to start with yourself and take responsibility for your inner state at any given moment. That means now. Ask yourself, "Is there negativity in me at this moment?" Then, become alert, attentive to your thoughts as well as your emotions. Watch out for the low-level unhappiness in whatever form, such as discontent, nervousness, being "fed up," and so on. Watch out for thoughts that appear to justify or explain this unhappiness but in reality cause it. The moment you become aware of a negative state within yourself, it does not mean you have failed. It means that you have succeeded. Until that awareness happens, there is identification with inner states, and such identification is ego.

With awareness comes disidentification from thoughts, emotions, and reactions. This is not to be confused with denial. The thoughts, emotions, or reactions are recognized, and in the moment of recognizing, disidentification happens automatically. Your sense of self, of who you are, then undergoes a shift: Before you were the thoughts, emotions, and reactions; now you are the awareness, the conscious Presence that witnesses those states.

Emotions and even thoughts become depersonalized through awareness. Their impersonal nature is recognized. There is no longer a self in them. They are just human emotions, human thoughts. Your entire personal history, which is ultimately no more than a story, a bundle of thoughts and emotions, becomes of secondary importance and no longer occupies the forefront of your consciousness. It no longer forms the basis for your sense of identity. You are the light of Presence, the awareness that is prior to and deeper than any thoughts and emotions.

Negativity is not intelligent. It is always of the ego.

Whenever you are in a negative state, there is something in you that wants the negativity, that perceives it as pleasurable, or that believes it will get you what you want. Otherwise, who would want to hang on to negativity, make themselves and others miserable, and create disease in the body? So, whenever there is negativity in you, if you can be aware at that moment that there is something in you that takes pleasure in it or believes it has a useful purpose, you are becoming aware of the ego directly. The moment this happens, your identity has shifted from ego to awareness. This means the ego is shrinking and awareness is growing.

If in the midst of negativity you are able to realize "At this moment I am creating suffering for myself" it will be enough to raise you above the limitations of conditioned egoic states and reactions. It will open up infinite possibilities which come to you when there is awareness — other vastly more intelligent ways of dealing with any situation. You will be free to let go of your unhappiness the moment you recognize it as unintelligent.

The more shared past there is in a relationship, the more present you need to be; otherwise, you will be forced to relive the past again and again.

A genuine relationship is one that is not dominated by the ego with its image-making and self-seeking. In a genuine relationship, there is an outward flow of open, alert attention toward the other person in which there is no wanting whatsoever. That alert attention is Presence. It is the prerequisite for any authentic relationship.

As you look at, listen to, touch, or help your child with this or that, you are alert, still, completely present, not wanting anything other than that moment as it is. In this way, you make room for Being. In that moment, if you are present, you are not a father or mother. You are the alertness, the stillness, the Presence that is listening, looking, touching, even speaking. You are the Being behind the doing.

I have been speaking of this with specific reference to the relationship with your child, but it equally applies, of course, to all relationships.

Doing is never enough if you neglect Being.

Most humans see only the outer forms, unaware of the inner essence, just as they are unaware of their own essence and identify only with their own physical and psychological form. Once there is a certain degree of Presence, of still and alert attention in your perceptions, however, you can sense the divine life essence, the one indwelling consciousness or spirit in every creature, every life-form, recognize it as one with your own essence and so love it as yourself.

When you meet with people, at work or wherever it may be, give them your fullest attention. You are no longer there primarily as a person, but as a field of awareness, of alert Presence. The original reason for interacting with the other person—buying or selling something, requesting or giving information, and so on—now becomes secondary. The field of awareness that arises between you becomes the primary purpose for the interaction. That space of awareness becomes more important than what you may be talking about, more important than physical or thought objects. The human *Being* becomes more important than the things of this world. It does not mean you neglect whatever needs to be done on a practical level. In fact, the doing unfolds not only more easily, but more powerfully when the dimension of Being is acknowledged and so becomes primary. The arising of that unifying field of awareness between human beings is the most essential factor in relationships on the new earth.

Forgiveness happens naturally when you see that your grievances have no purpose other than to strengthen a false sense of self, to keep the ego in place. The seeing is freeing. Jesus' teaching to "Forgive your enemies" is essentially about the undoing of one of the main egoic structures in the human mind.

There is only one perpetrator of evil on the planet: human unconsciousness. That realization is true forgiveness. With forgiveness, your victim identity dissolves, and your true power emerges—the power of Presence. Instead of blaming the darkness, you bring in the light.

Presence is a state of inner spaciousness. When you are present, you ask: How do I respond to the needs of this situation, of this moment? In fact, you don't even need to ask the question. You are still, alert, open to what is. You bring a new dimension into the situation: space. Then you look and you listen. Thus you become one with the situation. When instead of reacting against a situation, you merge with it, the solution arises out of the situation itself. Actually, it is not you, the person, who is looking and listening, but the alert stillness itself. Then, if action is possible or necessary, you take action or rather right action happens through you. Right action is action that is appropriate to the whole. When the action is accomplished, the alert, spacious stillness remains. There is nobody who raises his arms in a gesture of triumph shouting a defiant "Yeah!" There is no one who says, "Look, I did that."

When you are present, when your attention is fully in the Now, that Presence will flow into and transform what you do. There will be quality and power in it. You are present when what you are doing is not primarily a means to an end (money, prestige, winning) but fulfilling in itself, when there is joy and aliveness in what you do. And, of course, you cannot be present unless you become friendly with the present moment. That is the basis for effective action, uncontaminated by negativity.

Chapter 8

CONSCIOUSNESS

The joy of Being is the joy of being conscious.

Consciousness is already conscious. It is the unmanifested, the eternal. The universe, however, is only gradually becoming conscious. Consciousness itself is timeless and therefore does not evolve. It was never born and does not die. When consciousness becomes the manifested universe, it appears to be subject to time and to undergo an evolutionary process. No human mind is capable of comprehending fully the reason for this process. But we can glimpse it within ourselves and become a conscious participant in it.

Consciousness is the intelligence, the organizing principle behind the arising of form. Consciousness has been preparing forms for millions of years so that it can express itself through them in the manifested.

Although the unmanifested realm of pure consciousness could be considered another dimension, it is not separate from this dimension of form. Form and formlessness interpenetrate. The unmanifested flows into this dimension as awareness, inner space, Presence. How does it do that? Through the human form that becomes conscious and thus fulfills its destiny.

Consciousness incarnates into the manifested dimension, that is to say, it becomes form. When it does so, it enters a dreamlike state. Intelligence remains, but consciousness becomes unconscious of itself. It loses itself in form, becomes identified with forms. This could be described as the descent of the divine into matter.

On our planet, the human ego represents the final stage of universal sleep, the identification of consciousness with form. It was a necessary stage in the evolution of consciousness.

The next step in human evolution is not inevitable, but for the first time in the history of our planet, it can be a conscious choice. Who is making that choice? You are. And who are you? Consciousness that has become conscious of itself.

The human brain is a highly differentiated form through which consciousness enters this dimension. It contains approximately one hundred billion nerve cells (called neurons), about the same number as there are stars in our galaxy, which could be seen as a macrocosmic brain. The brain does not create consciousness, but consciousness created the brain, the most complex physical form on earth, for its expression. When the brain gets damaged, it does not mean you lose consciousness. It means consciousness can no longer use that form to enter this dimension. You cannot lose consciousness because it is, in essence, who you are. You can only lose something that you have, but you cannot lose something that you are.

Although you cannot know consciousness, you can become conscious of it as yourself. You can sense it directly in any situation, no matter where you are. You can sense it here and now as your very Presence, the inner space in which the words on this page are perceived and become thoughts. It is the underlying I Am. The words you are reading and thinking are the foreground, and the I Am is the substratum, the underlying background to every experience, thought, feeling.

Spiritual realization is to see clearly that what I perceive, experience, think, or feel is ultimately not who I am, that I cannot find myself in all those things that continuously pass away.

The Buddha was probably the first human being to see this clearly, and so *anata* (no self) became one of the central points of his teaching. And when Jesus said, "Deny thyself," what he meant was: Negate (and thus undo) the illusion of self. If the self—ego—were truly who I am, it would be absurd to "deny" it.

What remains is the light of consciousness in which perceptions, experiences, thoughts, and feelings come and go. That is Being, that is the deeper, true I. When I know myself as that, whatever happens in my life is no longer of absolute but only of relative importance. I honor it, but it loses its absolute seriousness, its heaviness.

The only thing that ultimately matters is this: Can I sense my essential Beingness, the I Am, in the background of my life at all times? To be more accurate, can I sense the I Am that I Am at this moment? Can I sense my essential identity as consciousness itself? Or am I losing myself in what happens, losing myself in the mind, in the world?

When forms that you had identified with, that gave you your sense of self, collapse or are taken away, it can lead to a collapse of the ego, since ego is identification with form. When there is nothing to identify with anymore, who are you? When forms around you die or death approaches, your sense of Beingness, of I Am, is freed from its entanglement with form: Spirit is released from its imprisonment in matter. You realize your essential identity as formless, as an all-pervasive Presence, of Being prior to all forms, all identifications. You realize your true identity as consciousness itself, rather than what consciousness had identified with. That is the peace of God.

I want to know the mind of God," Einstein said. "The rest are details." What is the mind of God? Consciousness. What does it mean to know the mind of God? To be aware. What are the details? Your outer purpose, and whatever happens outwardly.

It has been said: "Stillness is the language God speaks, and everything else is a bad translation." Becoming conscious of stillness whenever we encounter it in our lives will connect us with the formless and timeless dimension within ourselves, that which is beyond thought, beyond ego. It may be the stillness that pervades the world of nature, or the stillness in your room in the early hours of the morning, or the silent gaps in between sounds. Stillness has no form—that is why through thinking we cannot become aware of it. Thought is form. Being aware of stillness means to be still. To be still is to be conscious without thought. You are never more essentially, more deeply, yourself than when you are still. When you are still, you are who you were before you temporarily assumed this physical and mental form called a person. You are also who you will be when the form dissolves. When you are still, you are who you are beyond your temporal existence: consciousness—unconditioned, formless, eternal.

Chapter 9

THE INNER BODY

We have to enter the body to go beyond it and find out that we are not that.

Equating the physical sense-perceived body that is destined to grow old, wither, and die with "I" always leads to suffering sooner or later. To refrain from identifying with the body doesn't mean that you neglect, despise, or no longer care for it. If it is strong, beautiful, or vigorous, you can enjoy and appreciate those attributes—while they last. You can also improve the body's condition through right nutrition and exercise. If you don't equate the body with who you are, when beauty fades, vigor diminishes, or the body becomes incapacitated, this will not affect your sense of worth or identity in any way. In fact, as the body begins to weaken, the formless dimension, the light of consciousness, can shine more easily through the fading form.

Ego arises when your sense of Beingness, of "I Am," which is formless consciousness, gets mixed up with form. This is the meaning of identification. This is forgetfulness of Being, the primary error.

Although body-identification is one of the most basic forms of ego, the good news is that it is also the one that you can most easily go beyond. This is done not by trying to convince yourself that you are not your body, but by shifting your attention from the external form of your body and from thoughts about your body— beautiful, ugly, strong, weak, too fat, too thin—to the feeling of aliveness inside it. No matter what your body's appearance is on the outer level, beyond the outer form it is an intensely alive energy field.

Take two or three conscious breaths. Now see if you can detect a subtle sense of aliveness that pervades your entire inner body. Can you feel your body from within, so to speak? Sense briefly specific parts of your body. Feel your hands, then your arms, feet, and legs. Can you feel your abdomen, chest, neck, and head? What about your lips? Is there life in them? Then become aware again of the inner body as a whole. You may want to close your eyes initially for this practice, and once you can feel your body, open your eyes, look around, and continue to feel your body at the same time. You may find there is no need to close your eyes, that you can, in fact, feel your inner body as you read this.

Your inner body is not solid but spacious. It is not your physical form but the life that animates the physical form. It is the intelligence that created and sustains the body, simultaneously coordinating hundreds of different functions of such extraordinary complexity that the human mind can only understand a tiny fraction of it. When you become aware of it, what is really happening is that the intelligence is becoming aware of itself. It is the elusive "life" that no scientist has ever found because the consciousness that is looking for it *is it*.

If you are not familiar with "inner body" awareness, close your eyes for a moment and find out if there is life inside your hands. Don't ask your mind. It will say, "I can't feel anything." Probably it will also say, "Give me something more interesting to think about." So instead of asking your mind, go to the hands directly. By this I mean become aware of the subtle feeling of aliveness inside them. It is there. You just have to go there with your attention to notice it. You may get a slight tingling sensation at first, then a feeling of energy or aliveness. If you hold your attention in your hands for a while, the sense of aliveness will intensify. Some people won't even have to close their eyes. They will be able to feel their "inner hands" at the same time as they read this. Then go to your feet, keep your attention there for a minute or so, and begin to feel your hands and feet at the same time. Then incorporate other parts of the body—legs, arms, abdomen, chest, and so on—into that feeling until you are aware of the inner body as a global sense of aliveness, diffused throughout the body.

What I call the "inner body" isn't really the body anymore but life energy, the bridge between form and formlessness. Make it a habit to feel the inner body as often as you can. After a while, you won't need to close your eyes anymore to feel it. For example, see if you can feel the inner body whenever you listen to someone. It almost seems like a paradox: When you are in touch with the inner body, you are not identified with your body anymore, nor are you identified with your mind. This is to say, you are no longer identified with form but moving away from form-identification toward formlessness, which we may also call Being. It is your essence identity. Body awareness not only anchors you in the present moment, it is a doorway out of the prison that is the ego. It also strengthens the immune system and the body's ability to heal itself.

As much as possible in everyday life, use awareness of the inner body to create space. When waiting, when listening to someone, when pausing to look at the sky, a tree, a flower, your partner, or child, feel the aliveness within at the same time. This means part of your attention or consciousness remains formless, and the rest is available for the outer world of form. Whenever you "inhabit" your body in this way, it serves as an anchor for staying present in the Now. It prevents you from losing yourself in thinking, in emotions, or in external situations.

Your physical body, which is form, reveals itself as essentially formless when you go deeper into it. It becomes a doorway into inner space. Although inner space has no form, it is intensely alive. That "empty space" is life in its fullness, the unmanifested Source out of which all manifestation flows. The traditional word for that Source is God.

Chapter 10

ONENESS WITH
ALL LIFE

Underneath the surface appearance, everything is not only connected with everything else, but also with the Source of all life out of which it came. Even a stone, and more easily a flower or a bird, could show you the way back to God, to the Source, to yourself. When you look at it or hold it and *let it be* without imposing a word or mental label on it, a sense of awe, of wonder, arises within you. Its essence silently communicates itself to you and reflects your own essence back to you.

Why does the ego play roles? Because of one unexamined assumption, one fundamental error, one unconscious thought. That thought is: I am not enough. Other unconscious thoughts follow: I need to play a role in order to get what I need to be fully myself; I need to get more so that I can be more. But you cannot be more than you are because underneath your physical and psychological form, you are one with Life itself, one with Being. In form, you are and will always be inferior to some, superior to others. In essence, you are neither inferior nor superior to anyone. True self-esteem and true humility arise out of that realization. In the eyes of the ego, self-esteem and humility are contradictory. In truth, they are one and the same.

What "I" could there be apart from life, apart from Being? It is utterly impossible. So there is no such thing as "my life," and I don't *have* a life. I *am* life. I and life are one. It cannot be otherwise. So how could I lose my life? How can I lose something that I don't have in the first place? How can I lose something that I Am? It is impossible.

The Truth is inseparable from who you are. Yes, you *are* the Truth. The very Being that you are is Truth. Jesus tried to convey that when he said, "I am the way and the truth and the life."[6] These words are one of the most powerful and direct pointers to the Truth, if understood correctly. Jesus speaks of the innermost I Am, the essence identity of every man and woman, every life-form, in fact. He speaks of the life that you are. Some Christian mystics have called it the Christ within; Buddhists call it your Buddha nature; for Hindus, it is Atman, the indwelling God. When you are in touch with that dimension within yourself—and being in touch with it is your natural state, not some miraculous achievement—all your actions and relationships will reflect the oneness with all life that you sense deep within. This is love.

Acknowledging the good that is already in your life is the foundation for all abundance.

The source of all abundance is not outside you. It is part of who you are. However, start by acknowledging and recognizing abundance without. See the fullness of life all around you. The warmth of the sun on your skin, the display of magnificent flowers outside a florist's shop, biting into a succulent fruit, or getting soaked in an abundance of water falling from the sky. The fullness of life is there at every step. The acknowledgment of that abundance that is all around you awakens the dormant abundance within. Then let it flow out. When you smile at a stranger, there is already a minute outflow of energy. You become a giver. Ask yourself often: "What can I give here; how can I be of service to this person, this situation?" You don't need to own anything to feel abundant, although if you feel abundant consistently things will almost certainly come to you. Abundance comes only to those who already have it.

The sapling doesn't want anything because it is at one with the totality, and the totality acts through it. "Look at the lilies of the field, how they grow" said Jesus, "they toil not, neither do they spin. Yet even Solomon in all his glory was not arrayed like one of these."[7] We could say that the totality—Life—wants the sapling to become a tree, but the sapling doesn't see itself as separate from life and so wants nothing for itself. It is one with what Life wants. That's why it isn't worried or stressed. And if it has to die prematurely, it dies with ease. It is as surrendered in death as it is in life. It senses, no matter how obscurely, its rootedness in Being, the formless and eternal one Life.

Whenever tragic loss occurs, you either resist or you yield. Some people become bitter or deeply resentful; others become compassionate, wise, and loving. Resistance is an inner contraction, a hardening of the shell of the ego. You are closed. Yielding means inner acceptance of what is. You are open to life.

When you yield internally, when you surrender, a new dimension of consciousness opens up. If action is possible or necessary, your action will be in alignment with the whole and supported by creative intelligence, the unconditioned consciousness. Circumstances and people then become helpful, cooperative. Coincidences happen. If no action is possible, you rest in the peace and inner stillness that come with surrender. You rest in God.

When I no longer confuse who I am with a temporary form of "me," then the dimension of the limitless and the eternal — God — can express itself through "me" and guide "me." It also frees me from dependency on form. However, a purely intellectual recognition or belief that "I am not this form" does not help. The all-important question is: At this moment, can I sense the presence of inner space, which really means, can I sense my own Presence, or rather, the Presence that I Am?

Ask yourself, "Am I aware not only of what is happening at this moment, but also of the Now itself as the living timeless inner space in which everything happens?"

If peace is really what you want, then you will choose peace. If peace mattered to you more than anything else and if you truly knew yourself to be spirit rather than a little me, you would remain nonreactive and absolutely alert when confronted with challenging people or situations. You would immediately accept the situation and thus become one with it rather than separate yourself from it. Then out of your alertness would come a response. Who you are (consciousness), not who you think you are (a small me), would be responding. It would be powerful and effective and would make no person or situation into an enemy.

Being at one with what *is*, at one with the present moment, doesn't mean you no longer initiate change or become incapable of taking action. But the motivation to take action comes from a deeper level, not from egoic wanting or fearing. Inner alignment with the present moment opens your consciousness and brings it into alignment with the whole, of which the present moment is an integral part. The whole, the totality of life, then acts through you.

Life will give you whatever experience is most helpful for the evolution of your consciousness. How do you know this is the experience you need? Because this is the experience you are having at this moment.

How to be at peace now? By making peace with the present moment. The present moment is the field on which the game of life happens. It cannot happen anywhere else. Once you have made peace with the present moment, see what happens, what you can do or choose to do, or rather what life does through you.

There are three words that convey the secret of the art of living, the secret of all success and happiness: One With Life. Being one with life is being one with Now. You then realize that you don't live your life, but life lives you. Life is the dancer, and you are the dance.

God is the One Life in and beyond the countless forms of life. Love implies duality: lover and beloved, subject and object. So love is the recognition of oneness in the world of duality. This is the birth of God into the world of form. Love makes the world less worldly, less dense, more transparent to the divine dimension, the light of consciousness itself.

NOTES

1   1 Corinthians 3:19 (New Revised Standard Version)

2   Matthew 5:3 (New Revised Standard Version)

3   Ecclesiastes 1:8 (New Revised Standard Version)

4   Luke 17:20–21 (New Revised Standard Version)

5   Emerson, Ralph Waldo, "Circles," in Ralph Waldo Emerson: Selected Lectures, Essays, and Poems (New York: Bantam Classics).

6   John 14:6 (New Revised Standard Version)

7   Matthew 6:28–29 (New Revised Standard Version)

Are you ready to put aside ego and be awakened?

Right now the world is filled with angry, raging egos. But there is a better way and in *A New Earth*, Eckhart Tolle provides the spiritual framework for all of us to move beyond ourselves in order to make this world a better, more evolved place to live.

Shattering modern ideas of ego and entitlement, self and society, Tolle lifts the veil of fear that has hung over us during this new millennium, and reveals a path to happiness and health that every reader can follow.

From the bestselling author of *The Power of Now*.

'A wake-up call for the entire planet. *A New Earth* helps us to stop creating our own suffering and obsessing over the past and what the future might be, and to put ourselves in the now'
Oprah Winfrey

'An otherworldly genius'
Chris Evans' *BBC Radio 2*

Praise for Eckhart Tolle

'I keep Eckhart's book at my bedside. I think it's essential spiritual teaching. It's one of the most valuable books I've ever read' Oprah

'I would do anything to be anywhere in the vicinity of Eckhart Tolle' Jim Carrey

'A gentle journey, one that could take you to a spectacular and very special place of new awareness and deeper understanding' Neale Donald Walsh, author of *Conversations with God*

'One of the best books to come along in years. Every sentence rings with truth and power – the power to bring you into the gap, the space between our thoughts, where we find – as Eckhart so beautifully puts it – deep serenity, stillness, and a sacred Presence' Deepak Chopra, author of *The Seven Spiritual Laws of Success*

Here is some free space for you to fill with your own observations, feelings and insights . . .

....

....

....

....

....

....

....

....

....

....

....

....

....

....